America, My Country
Native Peoples

The Nez Perce

By Doraine Bennett

STATE
STANDARDS
PUBLISHING®

Your State • Your Standards • Your Grade Level

Dear Educators, Librarians and Parents . . .

Thank you for choosing books from State Standards Publishing! This book supports state Departments of Educations' standards for elementary level social studies and has been measured by the ATOS Readability Formula for Books (Accelerated Reader), the Lexile Framework for Reading, and the Fountas & Pinnell Benchmark Assessment System for Guided Reading. Photographs and/or illustrations, captions, and other design elements have been included to provide supportive visual messaging to enhance text comprehension. Glossary and Word Index sections introduce key new words and help young readers develop skills in locating and combining information. "Think With Bagster" questions provide teachers and parents with tools for additional learning activities and critical thinking development. We wish you all success in using this book to meet your student or child's learning needs.

Jill Ward, President

Publisher
State Standards Publishing, LLC
1788 Quail Hollow
Hamilton, GA 31811, USA
1.866.740.3056, www.statestandardspublishing.com

Cataloging-in-Publication Data
Bennett, Doraine.
    The Nez Perce / Doraine Bennett.
        p. cm. -- (America, my country Native Peoples)
    Includes index.
    ISBN 978-1-935884-91-0 (lib. bdg.)
    ISBN 978-1-935884-97-2 (pbk.)
    1. Nez Perce Indians--Juvenile literature.   I. Title.
    973--dc23
                    2012948405

About the Author

Doraine Bennett has a degree in professional writing from Columbus State University in Columbus, Georgia, and has been writing and teaching writing for over twenty years. She is a published author of numerous books for children, as well as magazine articles for both children and adults. She is the editor of the National Infantry Association's *Infantry Bugler* magazine. Doraine enjoys reading and flower gardening. She lives in Georgia with her husband, Cliff.

Editor's Note:

1877 Flight – Sources vary on the length of the flight route. The official Nez Perce National Historic Trail stretches approximately 1,170 miles.
Attire – The Nez Perce are historically known to have adopted attire from Plains Indian tribes through their travels, which may be reflected in non-photographic, fine art images. Items such as claw necklaces, skin shields and helmets, feather bonnets, and beadwork are well documented, as are later beaded hide vests. (See Nez Perce National Historical Park)

1 2 3 4 5 – CG – 17 16 15 14 13

Table of Contents

Hi, I'm Bagster! Let's learn about Native Peoples.

MY STATE

Heart of the Monster is where Coyote left the monster's heart.

The Nez Perce say they have been in the Pacific Northwest since "time immemorial," or the very distant past.

From the Heart of the Monster

The Nez Perce call themselves Nimi'ipuu (nee-mee-poo). It means "real people" or "we the people." Explorers of the American West named them Nez Perce, a French word that means "pierced nose." No one knows why they used this name, because the Nez Perce did not practice nose piercing. Some historians think the explorers may have mistaken them for another tribe.

The Nez Perce language is a difficult one. The words are very long, and they have consonant sounds that do not exist in English. Try to say, "How are you?" *Ta'c meeywi, manaa wees?* An important word in the Nez Perce language is *m'a min* (mah-min). It means horse.

The Nez Perce say they have been in the Pacific Northwest since "time **immemorial**," or the very distant past. Their creation story tells of a battle between a spirit being called Coyote and a terrible monster. The monster had eaten all the creatures of the land. Coyote tricked the monster into eating him. Once inside the monster, Coyote cut open the monster's body and let all the creatures escape. Then Coyote killed the monster and scattered pieces of his body. Each piece became a nation of native people. Coyote left the monster's heart near present-day Kamiah, Idaho, and sprinkled its blood in the countryside nearby to create the Nez Perce. The Nez Perce were a peaceful people, but when they had to fight they were fierce warriors.

Love for the Land

The Nez Perce lived where present-day Idaho, Oregon, and Washington meet. The Bitterroot Mountains of Idaho, part of the Rocky Mountain Range, formed the eastern boundary of their main territory. The western boundary was the Blue Mountains of Washington and Oregon, part of the Cascade Mountain Range. At times, their territory extended further into these three states, and into what is now Montana and Wyoming.

Three major rivers ran through Nez Perce territory: the Snake River, the Clearwater River, and the Salmon River. The area is part of the Columbia Plateau. The land there is a mixture of tree-covered mountains, flat-topped **plateaus**, and flowering **prairies**. The rivers cut deep **canyons** into the land. Hell's Canyon on the Snake River is the deepest canyon in North America. It is even deeper than the Grand Canyon.

Trees and shrubs like Lewis's mock orange, willow, and cottonwood grow in the valleys of the plateau. Tall pines grow on the plateaus, and evergreens on the mountains. The Nez Perce had great respect for the land, and still do today.

MAP KEY
- ■ Main Territory
- ■ Extended Territory
- — Columbia Plateau

Hell's Canyon on the Snake River is the deepest canyon in North America.

The Columbia Plateau is a land of tree-covered mountains, flat-topped plateaus, and flowering prairies.

7

In spring, men traveled to the rivers to fish.

In summer, the Nez Perce lived in temporary camps higher up, where the heat was not so severe.

8

Moving with the Seasons

The temperature and climate of the Nez Perce homeland could change drastically as the land changed. The mountains were often windy and cold. Winter snows drained into the rivers, providing water for the plants and animals. Temperatures on the high meadows were mild. The sheltered valleys and deep canyons could be terribly hot in the dry summers.

During the winter, the Nez Perce lived in permanent settlements in sheltered river valleys. They ate dried salmon and dried roots. When spring came, they were hungry for fresh food. The men traveled to the rivers to fish and the women dug for roots in the valleys and prairies. In summer they moved to higher areas and set up temporary camps where the heat was not so severe. The women gathered berries and the men hunted game animals like moose and bear for food. In late fall, they returned to their permanent villages along the rivers to fish and to store food for the coming winter.

The Nez Perce often caught salmon with a **weir**, or fish trap, that let the hunters catch many fish at once during the spring salmon runs. The men built a dam across the river with rocks, sticks, and logs. The weir forced the salmon to swim to the single opening in the dam, and into a cage-like basket. The fish could swim in, but they couldn't get out. The trap could be lifted out of the river and the fish dumped out for the women to clean, cook and dry.

Hunters and Gatherers

Nez Perce hunters tracked elk, deer, mountain sheep, and bear. Herds of antelope and bison, or buffalo, lived on the grasses of the Great Plains east of the Bitterroot Mountains. Small game birds called grouse nested in the mountains and on the plateau. Waterfowl like ducks and geese lived near the rivers. The Nez Perce hunted all of these for food.

Women gathered serviceberries, huckleberries, elderberries, and chokecherries, along with nuts and seeds. They dug the roots and bulbs from camas, kouse, and other plants. Camas and kouse were especially important because they could be dried for winter. The women ground the kouse to make soup or formed it into dried cakes for later use. The camas bulb, a type of lily, could be eaten raw, baked, or boiled. The women dug a pit in the ground and lined it with split wood and stones. Then they lit a fire in the pit. When the stones were hot, they put the fire out and laid camas roots wrapped in layers of grass on the hot stones. The camas cooked for two days. It tasted a little like a baked sweet potato. The cooked camas could be made into bread and stored for winter. The juice was a good cough syrup.

Camas once grew in vast prairies on the Columbia Plateau. In May, their purple blooms were said to make the prairie look like a lake. Today visitors can still enjoy the "Big Bloom" in May at Camas Prairie near Fairfield, Idaho.

Women dug the roots and bulbs from camas, kouse, and other plants.

Hunters tracked herds of antelope on the grasses of the Great Plains east of the Bitterroot Mountains.

12   In summer, the Nez Perce lived in tipis, like these.

Longhouses and Tipis

The Nez Perce lived in groups of extended families. Their main dwelling was a **longhouse**. The families would often dig a shallow, oval-shaped hole in the ground. Heavy log posts supported the roof. The women wove mats from cattails and tules, grasslike plants that grew in the marshy areas of the rivers. They used the mats to cover the A-shaped roof of the longhouse and piled dirt from the hole around the bottom. They also used the mats as mattresses for sleeping and spread on the ground as a table. As the family grew, the longhouse could be extended. Some longhouses were 100 feet long and held many families.

In summer when the Nez Perce traveled, they removed the grass mats from the longhouse roof. They packed the mats with their belongings and used them to make summer homes called **tipis**. Long poles were tied together, and other poles were laid against them. The grass mats were placed on the outside as covering. Later on, the Nez Perce replaced the grass mats with bison skins.

Longhouses were covered in mats made from cattails and tules.

Buckskin Clothes

Nez Perce men wore **breechcloths** and moccasins. They also wore leg coverings called leggings and fringed **buckskin** shirts. The soft buckskin leather was made from the skin of deer, elk, or sheep. In cold weather, they wore robes made from bison or elk skin. The robes were decorated with dyed porcupine quills, beads, bones, and paint. They wore a headband with a ring of feathers standing around the head.

Nez Perce women made their dresses from the skin of deer or sheep. The softer sheepskin was often preferred. They wore basket hats made from corn husks. The Nez Perce were famous for making a flat, twined wallet or bag from the Indian hemp plant that grew near rivers and streams. A well-made bag was woven so tightly that it would hold water.

Both men and women painted their faces. The designs and colors were different for war, religious ceremonies, and special celebrations.

Men sometimes wore a headband with a ring of feathers standing around the head.

Women's basket hats and wallets were tightly woven.

Nez Perce men wore breechcloths and moccasins. They also wore leggings and fringed buckskin shirts.

The Nez Perce used dugout canoes on rivers and streams.

How did the land and its resources shape the Nez Perce way of life?

Nez Perce Appaloosas were fast and strong.

Getting Around

Most historians agree that the Spanish explorers brought horses to the Americas. Once the Nez Perce obtained horses, they could travel faster and farther than before. They began to cross over the Bitterroot Mountains to follow the bison herds. They hunted bison for food and used bison skins for clothing and shelter.

The Nez Perce had large herds of Appaloosa horses. Appaloosas are known for their coats. Many are leopard-spotted. The Nez Perce learned to breed the horses by choosing the best of the herd. Nez Perce Appaloosas were fast and strong.

The Nez Perce carried their possessions on a sort of sled, called a **travois** (trah-voy). Two long poles were hooked to a horse with a collar. Sometimes skins were attached to the poles like a hammock with the back end dragging across the ground. The Nez Perce used the travois to transport their belongings when they moved from place to place. They carved **dugout** canoes for use on the rivers and streams.

A wild Appaloosa is a **natural resource**. It comes directly from nature. The man who trains it is a **human resource**. The trained Appaloosa would then be a **capital resource** the man can use for transportation or trading.

White Men Arrive

In 1803 President Thomas Jefferson bought 828,000 square miles of land from France. The **Louisiana Purchase** stretched from the Mississippi River west to the Rocky Mountains. Jefferson hired Meriwether Lewis and William Clark to explore the land and make a map. When the Lewis and Clark expedition crossed the rugged Bitterroot Mountains, they used the same trail the Native Americans used. The men were nearly starved. Their supplies had run out. The Indians welcomed them into their camp and gave them food. The explorers called these Indians the Nez Perce. These were the first white men the Nez Perce had seen.

Lewis and Clark traded with the Nez Perce for fresh horses and supplies. The Nez Perce told them how to cross the Columbia Plateau to reach the Columbia River. The river would take them to the Pacific Ocean, but they would need canoes. The Nez Perce helped Lewis and Clark choose the best trees for building their canoes. When they were finished, Lewis and Clark left their horses in the care of the Nez Perce and continued their journey to the coast.

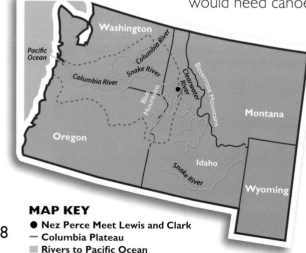

MAP KEY
- Nez Perce Meet Lewis and Clark
- Columbia Plateau
- Rivers to Pacific Ocean

18

The Nez Perce welcomed Lewis and Clark into their camp.

How did explorers and settlers affect the Nez Perce?

A steady stream of settlers began traveling the Oregon Trail toward the west coast.

Settlers Looking for Land

On the return trip, Lewis and Clark stopped at the Nez Perce camp to collect their horses. Snow in the Bitterroot Mountains forced them to stay nearly a month. They hunted, fished, and entertained the people. The Nez Perce had never seen magnets, a spyglass, or a watch. When the pass through the mountains was clear, Lewis and Clark left the Nez Perce with a promise of peace from the American government. It was a promise that would be broken.

After Lewis and Clark's encounter with the Nez Perce, trappers and fur traders arrived in the Northwest. Missionaries, a kind of priest, came to tell the Nez Perce about the Christian religion. Soon a steady stream of settlers began traveling the **Oregon Trail** toward the west coast. As more settlers arrived, disagreements over the land arose. The Nez Perce signed a **treaty** with the United States in 1855. The treaty gave the government a portion of the Nez Perce land in exchange for cash and the rights to continue hunting and fishing on it. The remaining Nez Perce land was set aside as a **reservation** where the Nez Perce people could live.

MAP KEY
■ **Nez Perce Territory**
■ **Extended Territory**
■ **Lewis & Clark Trail**
■ **Oregon Trail**

The Problem of Gold

In the 1860s, gold was discovered on Nez Perce lands. Miners rushed to the gold fields. They didn't care that the land belonged to the Nez Perce people. There were many arguments over the land. The U.S. government wanted the Nez Perce to sign a new treaty. This treaty would reduce the size of their reservation to a small fraction of the amount of land promised to them. Some Nez Perce chiefs signed the treaty. But Old Chief Joseph from a Nez Perce **band**, or tribal group, in Oregon refused and walked out of the meeting. Chiefs from four other bands also refused to sign the treaty. They soon became known as the nontreaty bands.

Many Nez Perce moved to the reservation. Living there forced them to give up some of their traditional ways. Instead of hunting and gathering their food, many became farmers. They raised grain crops like wheat and barley. They had to send their children to a school established by the government. Still, the nontreaty bands of Nez Perce refused to move.

Five bands refused to sign the treaty. Their chiefs were:
Joseph and Ollokot *(oh-luh-kut)*
Looking Glass
White Bird
Toohoolhoolzote *(tah-hool-hool-shoot)*
Husis Kute *(hush-hush-cute)*

Nez Perce on the reservation had to give up their traditional ways.

Miners rushed into Nez Perce lands when gold was discovered.

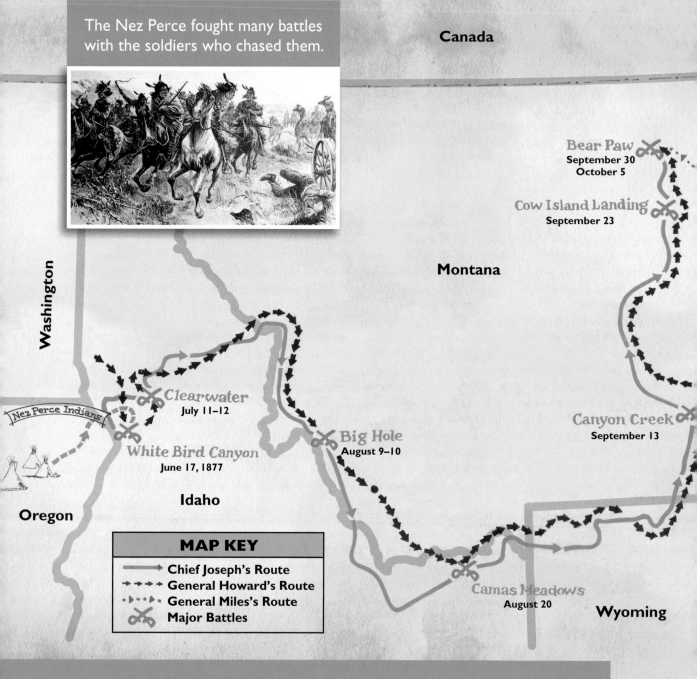

The Nez Perce fought many battles with the soldiers who chased them.

Canada

Bear Paw
September 30
October 5

Cow Island Landing
September 23

Montana

Washington

Nez Perce Indians

Clearwater
July 11–12

White Bird Canyon
June 17, 1877

Big Hole
August 9–10

Canyon Creek
September 13

Idaho

Oregon

MAP KEY
➤ Chief Joseph's Route
➤ General Howard's Route
➤ General Miles's Route
⚔ Major Battles

Camas Meadows
August 20

Wyoming

Nez Perce warriors fought the Army from Oregon to Montana.

The Nez Perce War

When Old Chief Joseph died, his son, who was also named Joseph, took over. The new Chief Joseph was well-educated and spoke English. The government told him he had thirty days to move his people onto the reservation. Chief Joseph realized his only choice was to move or go to war. He did not want his people killed, so he agreed to move.

Before the people could relocate, some younger members of Chief White Bird's band attacked a group of white men. Some of the white men were killed. There was nothing left to do but run.

Chief Joseph and the other nontreaty chiefs took about 250 warriors and about 500 women, children, and old men and headed toward Canada. They hoped they could find safety outside the United States. But Generals Oliver Howard, Nelson Miles, and the U.S. Army followed them. The Nez Perce traveled over 1,100 miles of mountains and prairies. They fought many battles with the soldiers who chased them. The Nez Perce won every battle. Finally when they were only forty miles from Canada, U.S. soldiers surrounded them near Bear Paw in Montana. After five days of fighting, the chiefs knew there was no hope of winning. The people were freezing cold and hungry. The warriors had lost the **Nez Perce War of 1877**.

Does this map give you clues about why the Nez Perce lost the war?

Surrender

Although some Nez Perce escaped, Chief Joseph surrendered and was captured. He told his captors to tell the people, "Hear me, my chiefs. I am tired. My heart is sick and sad. From where the sun now stands, I will fight no more forever." The Army generals promised the Nez Perce they could return to their homeland. Instead they were taken as prisoners of war to Kansas, then sent to Oklahoma. Their horses were taken away. Years later, some nontreaty Nez Perce were returned to the Lapwai Reservation in the Idaho territory. Chief Joseph was finally sent to the Colville Reservation in present-day Washington. He never returned to his homeland in Oregon and died on the reservation in 1904.

Americans were shocked that the small band of Nez Perce could outsmart and outfight U. S. Army soldiers for so long. There were many more soldiers than Nez Perce. The soldiers had better equipment and guns. But the Nez Perce warriors were skilled fighters. They moved quickly and carried out surprise attacks against the enemy. Today, soldiers in the Army still study the Nez Perce War to understand how the band held off the Army for so long. The Army learned many lessons about fighting wars from the Nez Perce. They still use these lessons in defending our country today.

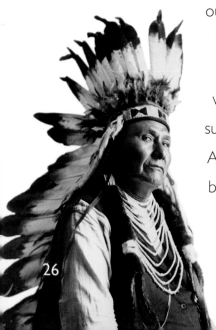

Chief Joseph

26

Chief Joseph died on the reservation in 1904.

Years later, some nontreaty Nez Perce were returned to the Lapwai Reservation in the Idaho territory.

Fish Hatcheries

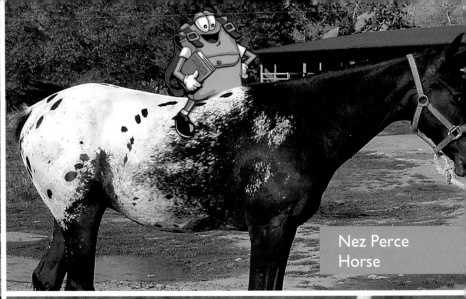

Nez Perce Horse

Chief Joseph Days Celebration

The Nez Perce Today

Today many Nez Perce live on reservations in Idaho and Washington. The Nez Perce Nation has its own government, laws, and police. In recent years, the tribe began a breeding program to develop the **Nez Perce Horse**. The new breed is a cross between an Appaloosa and an Akhal-Teke (ah-call tek-ee) horse from Asia, which is known for its endurance. Tribal programs teach Nez Perce children and youth about their history and how to raise the horses. The Nez Perce also operate fish hatcheries on the reservation. Hydroelectric plants and overharvesting had caused the salmon to die. The hatcheries are restoring the salmon to the rivers.

A "Chief Joseph Days" celebration is held in Oregon each year with parades and a rodeo. The Nez Perce remember their tribal history with ceremonies where they smoke pipes, sing, and pray. In an empty saddle ceremony, horses without riders are led around the field to honor the Nez Perce ancestors who died.

After the Nez Perce lost their horses, new owners did not breed them like the Nez Perce had. The Appaloosas lost strength and speed. The new Nez Perce breed has strength and endurance similar to the horses in Chief Joseph's time. Most still have the spotted coat the Nez Perce people love.

Glossary

band – A group of people who inhabit common territory, often based on kinship.

breechcloth – Cloth or animal skin hung from the waist and attached with a belt. Also called a loincloth.

buckskin – A strong, soft material made from the skin of deer or sheep.

canyon – A deep valley with steep sides, often with a stream flowing through it.

capital resources – Goods produced and used to make other goods and services.

dugout – A type of canoe made by hollowing out a log.

human resources – People working to produce goods and services.

immemorial – Originating in the distant past. Very old.

longhouse – A long dwelling, shared by many families.

Louisiana Purchase – A vast land purchase that extended the borders of United States territory from the Mississippi River to the Rocky Mountains and from the Gulf of Mexico to Canada.

natural resources – Things that come directly from nature that are useful to humans.

Nez Perce Horse – A horse produced by crossing an Appaloosa with an Akhal-Teke.

Nez Perce War of 1877 – A war fought between the Nez Perce and the U.S. government when nontreaty bands refused to give up their lands and move to a reservation.

Oregon Trail – A route across the central and western United States used by settlers.

plateau – A broad, flat area of high land.

prairie – A large area of level or rolling grassland.

reservation – An area of land set aside by the U.S. government for American Indians.

tipi – A cone-shaped tent used by American Indians as a home, usually made from animal skins or woven grasses.

travois – A type of sled mounted to an animal and used to carry goods.

treaty – A formal agreement between two or more countries or groups.

weir – A fence-like or basket-like trap used to catch fish.

Index

Editorial and Image Credits

Designer: Michael Sellner, Corporate Graphics, North Mankato, Minnesota
Consultant/Marketing Design: Alison Hagler, Basset and Becker Advertising, Columbus, Georgia

Images © copyright contributor unless otherwise specified.
Cover – "Top Gun" by Chuck Ren, GrayStonePress, Nashville, TN. **4/5** – Man: See Cover; Mound: Nez Perce National Historical Park. **6/7** – Plateau: D.S. Dugan/Wikipedia; Canyon: XWeinzar/Wikipedia. **8/9** – Horseback: North Wind Picture Archives; Fishing & Weir: NativeStock. **10/11** – Hunter: North Wind Picture Archives; Women: NativeStock; Camas: Charles Knowles/iStockphoto. **12/13** – Tipis: "Funeral Scaffold" by Karl Bodmer; Longhouses: NativeStock. **14/15** – Man & Hat: NativeStock; Group: Northwest Museum of Arts & Culture/Eastern Washington State Historical Society, Spokane, WA L9718.75. **16/17** – Riders: "Victory Dance" by Frederic Remington; Travois: "Indians on the Old Travois Trail" by Unknown; Dugout: Garry DeLong/Alamy. **18/19** – Lewis and Clark: New York Public Library/Historical and Public Figures: A general Portrait File to the 1920s/Stephen A. Schwarzman Building/Print Collection, Miriam and Ira D. Wallach Division of Art, Prints and Photographs. **20/21** – "Settlers Entering Ohio Territory" by Pyle. **22/23** – Panners: "Washing Gold" by Unknown; Children: Northwest Museum of Arts & Culture/Eastern Washington State Historical Society, Spokane, WA L94-52.93, E. G. Cummings **24/25** – Map: USDA-Forest Service/Wikipedia; Battle: Marino Govorova/iStockphoto. **26/27** – Group: NativeStock; Death: The Print Collector/Alamy; Chief Joseph: Smithsonian Bureau of American Ethnology/Wikipedia. **28/29** – Horse: JCI Nuria/Wikipedia; Hatchery: David R. Frazier Photolibrary Inc./Alamy; Rodeo: RedStormPhoto/Fotolia; Rider: NativeStock.

Think With Bagster

1. What are some of the ways the Nez Perce helped America grow?

2. Create a play with members of your class or write a letter about the talks between the U.S. government and Chief Joseph from the beginning to the end of the Nez Perce War.

3. A member of the Nez Perce tribe said this:

   "Our traditional relationship with the earth was more than just reverence for the land. It was knowing that every living thing had been placed here by the Creator and that we were part of a sacred relationship ... entrusted with the care and protection of our Mother Earth, we could not stand apart from our environment." – Elsie Maynard

   Explain what the Nez Perce believe about their relationship to the land and the environment. Do you believe we are responsible for these things today?

4. Draw a picture of an Appaloosa horse. How do you think the Appaloosa helped Chief Joseph and his warriors in the Nez Perce War?

5. Measure your classroom. If a Nez Perce longhouse was 100 feet long, how many of your classrooms would fit in it? Would you like to live in a longhouse? Why or why not?

6. On a map, trace the route the Nez Perce took toward Canada. Which states did they pass through?